LET'S VISIT
A Television Station

by Carol Freed

photography by Larry French

Troll Associates

Library of Congress Cataloging in Publication Data

Freed, Carol.
    Let's visit a television station.

    Summary: Reveals the many behind-the-scenes
activities involved in producing television programs
for the viewing audience and describes briefly the
work of the news editor, lighting technicians, director,
camera crew, and others.
    1. Television broadcasting—Juvenile literature.
[1. Television broadcasting.   2. Occupations]
I. French, Larry, ill.   II. Title.
PN1992.57.F74   1988   384.55´4´0973   87-3461
ISBN 0-8167-1165-8 (lib. bdg.)
ISBN 0-8167-1166-6 (pbk.)

The author and publisher wish to thank Leigh Curtin, Rosalind Miller and WOR-TV for their generous assistance
and cooperation.

Turning on the television is as easy as one, two, three! Just push a button or switch a knob. Then sit back and enjoy the show. But what goes on behind the scenes to get that show to you? Let's visit a television station and take a look at "the whole picture."

It's the baseball season! The television station sends a *camera crew* to the ball field. Cameras are positioned in different places all around the stadium. The cameras follow the action of the game by moving in different directions. A special device keeps the picture in focus even as the camera moves!

The *announcers* sit in a special booth high above the field. Most of the time they are heard but not seen as they describe the action of the game. But sometimes they interview players and coaches after the game is over. Then the people at home get to see what their sports announcers look like!

Most sports events such as baseball games are *live television programming*. What the camera crew sees through the camera, the viewer sees at home. And the home viewer sees it at just the moment it is happening on the field.

News shows are another example of live television programming. They are broadcast from a *studio* inside the TV station. The large, soundproof room is filled with lights, cameras, and special equipment. Most of the studio is dark. Only the *set* is lighted.

The *set* is the part of the studio that is seen on the TV screen. For a live newscast, the set is a table called the *anchor desk*. The people who sit behind the desk are called the *anchor people*. They read the news from a script on the desk or on the cameras in front of them.

At some TV stations the weather report is given outside of the studio. The camera crew must be prepared for rainy or snowy weather. Other members of the news team also report from outside the studio. On-the-scene reporters must cover the news from wherever it may happen!

Many people who work on a news show are
never seen on television. Most of these people
work in the newsroom next to the TV studio.

At the heart of this newsroom is a glass-
enclosed booth called the *assignment desk*. The
people who work here are *assignment editors*.
With the producers, they decide which stories
should be covered.

It's an assignment editor's job to find out what's going on in the world. They talk on the telephone to people called *sources*, who call in with important news tips. They read reports from wire services that print out the late-breaking news. They even listen to police band radios and the newscasts of other stations.

Once it is decided what news to cover, a team is assigned to each story. Most news teams are made up of a reporter and two members of the camera crew. A record of who is covering what is written on the *assignment board*.

13

While reporters gather information, newsroom writers prepare the show's scripts. They must be sure each story will fit in the time set aside to read it.

A graphics artist uses a computer to prepare colorful pictures. During the show, the pictures will appear on a screen behind the anchor people.

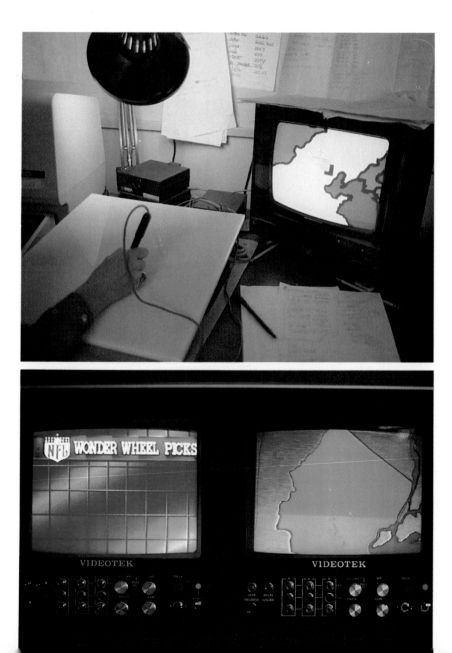

It's almost air time! The news team is back with a video tape of their news assignment. Now they must work with a *tape editor* to prepare their taped segment of the show. They must shorten the tape so it will fit into just a few minutes of air time.

Most of the shows on television are taped
before they are shown. Some television stations
have several studios working at once. While
the news is being broadcast live, a children's
show is being taped.

Actors study their scripts while they wait to
go before the cameras. They want to make
sure they will say their lines without a single
mistake. The clown will do tricks with an
acrobatic dog once he is on the set.

Lights! Camera! Action! The show is about to begin. When the cameras start rolling, the children act as if they were on live TV. They may laugh at the clown, applaud for the dog, or even sing a song. When the taped show airs at a later date, they can see themselves on TV.

Many people work behind the scenes to bring a program to you. It's the job of the *stage manager* to make sure everything goes smoothly in the studio. He tells the crew when to put props like balloons, and books, and toys on the set. The *lighting technicians* make sure the lights give the set a beautiful glow. And the camera crew knows just where to move. The director gives them instructions.

The *director* sits in a special booth known as the *control room*. He can see what's going on in the studio by looking at the many monitors. He decides which camera angles provide the best view of the set. Then he tells the camera crew where to move to get the best possible pictures.

Often, more than one camera is used to tape a TV show. The director decides which camera provides the best shot at a particular time. He tells the *technical director* which camera he wants to tape a scene on the set. The technical director then controls which camera is on by pressing buttons on the *switcher.*

In the booth beside the control room sits the *audio technician*. He makes sure that the sound is clear and that it's neither too loud nor too soft. Like other workers behind the scenes, he wants everything to be just right!

Once a tape is made it is later played in the *video tape room* at the station. The video tape room has lots of different machines.

Many technicians work in the video tape room to be sure that everything runs smoothly. The technicians check monitors, thread tapes into machines, and do many other jobs.

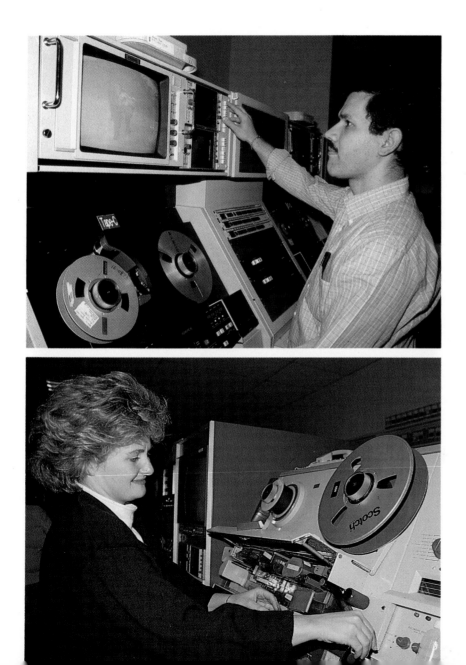

Every television station has a huge *media library* where tapes of their programs are kept. They even have tapes of old, old shows that are no longer seen on TV. Sometimes stations rent *syndicated programs* to show on the air. These are tapes of shows that were made outside of their studios.

With so many shows going on the air, it's a wonder that things run so smoothly. Every second of air time is carefully planned and entered into a computer. A master schedule, or *log,* is then printed and distributed around the station.

The technician in charge of commercials must know the log inside out! The commercials for each day are taken from their shelves and rolled on a movable rack. They will then be placed in a *tape-cart machine*. Twenty-two can fit in at one time.

The commercials come in little red boxes. The technician must check the titles on each one. After looking at the log, he puts the commercials into the machine in the right order. They are now ready to be played automatically during commercial breaks in each program.

Just as each studio has a control room, the station has a *master control room*. There are many devices in the room, including a board called the *master switcher.* People who work here can monitor everything that goes on all over the station. They make sure that the proper pictures and sound get into your home.

But how does a show make its way from the station into people's homes? Signals are sent out from the station's *transmitting antenna*. They travel through the air and arrive as a picture with sound on the TV screen.

Watching TV is easy—and it's fun! There are so many things to see! But a lot of hard work goes into bringing a television program to you. Now that you've got "the whole picture" of what happens in a television station, you'll probably never look at your favorite shows in quite the same way again!